GRIEF

GRIEF

Biblical

TRUTHS

— *that* —

Bring Healing

PUBLISHING GROUP

NASHVILLE, TENNESSEE

CONTENTS

CONTENTS

Somewhere along the line, the Bible attracted a reputation for being both irrelevant and impossible to understand. Out of touch as well as out of reach. Yet while conclusions like these continue to persist, so does human need for the Bible to be everything God affirms it to be: "living and effective" (Hebrews 4:12), its message "very near you, in your mouth and in your heart" (Deuteronomy 30:14).

If families and friends are to live together in unity . . . if lives are to be whole and fruitful in heart and mind . . . if tragedy and loss and disappointment and confusion are to be survived . . . no, not merely survived but transformed into peace and power and a purposeful way forward . . . you need a Word that is here and now and able to be grasped. You need to "know the truth," because "the truth will set you free" (John 8:32).

That's why you picked up this book. As the grief in your life becomes overwhelming, you need to take a step back and soak in God's Word.

Filled with Scriptures that speak personally to you this little book is further proof that God intends His Word to share living space with your present reality. Always in touch. Always within reach. No matter where you are, or what you are going through, allow this book to help direct you to the Scriptures you need most.

Sometimes it can feel like the entire world is against us. Everything is going wrong, and we are trapped in our circumstances. But grief is not the end. God is for us; and if that is true who can be against us? Our eternal reassurance in the face of conflict, rejection, uncertainty, and loss is that God's love for us is constant. No matter what kind of grief you find yourself in, let these verses reassure you of the one who is always on your side.

But the LORD said to Samuel, "Do not look at his appearance or his stature because I have rejected him. Humans do not see what the LORD sees, for humans see what is visible, but the LORD sees the heart."

    1 Samuel 16:7

———

Everyone the Father gives me will come to me, and the one who comes to me I will never cast out.

    John 6:37

But God proves his own love for us in that while we were still sinners, Christ died for us.
Romans 5:8

———

If God is for us, who is against us?
Romans 8:31

———

Peter began to speak: "Now I truly understand that God doesn't show favoritism, but in every nation the person who fears him and does what is right is acceptable to him.
Acts 10:34–35

Father, I am lost in grief. I am at the point where I feel trapped in doubt and despair. Thank You for Your constant presence through the valley, and for Your acceptance of me into Your family. Turn on the light so that I can find my way out of this place of despair. Continue to hold me in Your arms and never let me go. Amen

ANGER

Anger at yourself, anger at the world, anger at God; there are countless occasions for anger to rear its ugly head. It's an emotion that we all feel and tend to feel toward those we care about the most. The key is not to act out in anger, but to discover the root of your anger and work through the grief that is left when your anger subsides. When you are overcome with emotion, never let anger be in the driver's seat. It will only lead you deeper into grief.

Refrain from anger and give up your rage; do not be agitated—it can only bring harm.

Psalm 37:8

———

A patient person shows great understanding, but a quick-tempered one promotes foolishness.

Proverbs 14:29

———

A gentle answer turns away anger, but a harsh word stirs up wrath.

Proverbs 15:1

"But I tell you, everyone who is angry with his brother or sister will be subject to judgment. Whoever insults his brother or sister, will be subject to the court. Whoever says, 'You fool!' will be subject to hellfire."

    Matthew 5:22

————

Be angry and do not sin. Don't let the sun go down on your anger, and don't give the devil an opportunity.

    Ephesians 4:26–27

Lord, right now I am holding on to anger in my heart. Wipe this anger out of me. Give me the peace and patience that I need to forgive. Remind me daily of the forgiveness that You have given me. I'm afraid that if I let go of my anger I will not have anything left. I desire to love well, but I know I cannot do this without Your guiding hand. Grant me the wisdom to know how to handle this situation in love, and to know that letting go of my anger will not leave me empty, but give room for You to fill. Amen

Anxiety can come up in every part of our lives. Beneath our anxieties is a need to feel in control. Control in the midst of grief is impossible, and trying to hold on to it will only leave you scrambling. Our peace is found in knowing that the Creator of the universe holds us safely in the palm of His hand and will protect us no matter the situation in which we land. Release control to God, and allow yourself to be free in His hand.

"Therefore I tell you: Don't worry about your life, what you will eat or what you will drink; or about your body, what you will wear. Isn't life more than food and the body more than clothing? Consider the birds of the sky: They don't sow or reap or gather into barns, yet your heavenly Father feeds them. Aren't you worth more than they? Can any of you add one moment to his life-span by worrying?"

Matthew 6:25–27

———

Don't worry about anything, but in everything, through prayer and petition with thanksgiving, present your requests to God. And the peace of God, which surpasses all understanding, will guard your hearts and minds in Christ Jesus.

Philippians 4:6–7

"Peace I leave with you. My peace I give to you. I do not give to you as the world gives. Don't let your heart be troubled or fearful."

   John 14:27

———

For God has not given us a spirit of fear, but one of power, love, and sound judgment.

   2 Timothy 1:7

———

Humble yourselves, therefore, under the mighty hand of God, so that he may exalt you at the proper time, casting all your cares on him, because he cares about you.

   1 Peter 5:6–7

Heavenly Father, no matter how much I wish it was not true, there are things that are outside of my control. I worry that I am not doing enough, or too much, or am not fully known or fully loved. I feel lost without some kind of control. Help me to leave my anxieties at Your feet. I entrust to You my anxieties, knowing that Your peace will guard my heart and mind. Amen

All of creation is ablaze with the beauty of the Lord. But sometimes it is easier to see than others. When you are going through a difficult situation it is hard to see beauty. It is hard to imagine that anything will ever look beautiful again. And that is exactly when you need to see the beauty of God the most. Be intentional—look for it in sunsets, the night stars, and blooms of flowers. Find beauty in the midst of your grief, and remember that God is with you.

You are absolutely beautiful, my darling; there is no imperfection in you.

   Song of Solomon 4:7

———

I will praise you because I have been remarkably and wondrously made. Your works are wondrous, and I know this very well.

   Psalm 139:14

———

Charm is deceptive and beauty is fleeting, but a woman who fears the LORD will be praised.

   Proverbs 31:30

I have asked one thing from the LORD; *it is what I desire: to dwell in the house of the* LORD *all the days of my life, gazing on the beauty of the* LORD *and seeking him in his temple.*

    Psalm 27:4

———

Don't let your beauty consist of outward things like elaborate hairstyles and wearing gold jewelry, but rather what is inside the heart—the imperishable quality of a gentle and quiet spirit, which is of great worth in God's sight.

    1 Peter 3:3–4

Heavenly Father, I thank You and praise You for the beauty You have poured out on this earth, which heals and blesses the hearts that behold it. I am lost and need Your beauty to pull me back. Show me Your wondrous creation, and help me to never lose sight of the beauty that surrounds me, even in the darkest places. Amen

In the midst of grief, it feels impossible to remember the blessings that God has placed in our lives. But even in the darkness, He is there. We can experience deep joy when we take notice of the abundant blessings in our lives and praise and thank the Lord for such bountiful grace, even in the midst of sorrow. While grieving, remember the provisions that God has given You.

"May the LORD bless you and protect you; may the LORD make his face shine on you and be gracious to you; may the LORD look with favor on you and give you peace."

Numbers 6:24–26

———

Indeed, we have all received grace upon grace from his fullness, for the law was given through Moses; grace and truth came through Jesus Christ.

John 1:16–17

———

And God is able to make every grace overflow to you, so that in every way, always having everything you need, you may excel in every good work.

2 Corinthians 9:8

Blessed is the God and Father of our Lord Jesus Christ, who has blessed us with every spiritual blessing in the heavens in Christ.

Ephesians 1:3

———

And my God will supply all your needs according to his riches in glory in Christ Jesus.

Philippians 4:19

Heavenly Father, I thank You and praise You for all the ways You have shown me mercy and grace, and I ask for the blessing of Your presence throughout this day. I know that I could not get through this time of grief without Your outpouring of grace. Give me reminders today of Your goodness. Amen

Everyone responds to grief differently. One person may seek out help, while another may attempt to escape notice. But no one can get through grief alone. We all need some form of help, whether it is directly from God, or Him flowing through other people. Be honest with those who love you when you need help. Look for ways to love those who are grieving.

"I give you a new command: Love one another. Just as I have loved you, you are also to love one another. By this everyone will know that you are my disciples, if you love one another."
    John 13:34–35

———

Carry one another's burdens; in this way you will fulfill the law of Christ.
    Galatians 6:2

Therefore, as we have opportunity, let us work for the good of all, especially for those who belong to the household of faith.

Galatians 6:10

———

Everyone should look out not only for his own interests, but also for the interests of others.

Philippians 2:4

Father God, help me reflect Your gracious patience and unfailing love. Show me ways to love and care for my friends well. It is so easy for me to take my relationships for granted and forget that if they are neglected they could easily disappear. Show me ways today that I can show my friends how much I care for them. Help me to see the ways in which they care for me, and let me not ever take for granted having them in my life. Amen

Change is frightening. Whether you are mourning the loss of a loved one, preparing to leave a home you love, searching for a job, or even lost in a sadness you do not fully understand, grief marks a kind of change—both seen and unseen. No matter what that change is the presence of God goes before you preparing the way. Have confidence that on the other side of this change, no matter what the new world looks like, God will be there.

There is an occasion for everything, and a time for every activity under heaven.

    Ecclesiastes 3:1

———

"Do not remember the past events, pay no attention to things of old. Look, I am about to do something new; even now it is coming. Do you not see it? Indeed, I will make a way in the wilderness, rivers in the desert."

    Isaiah 43:18–19

"Because I, the LORD, have not changed, you descendants of Jacob have not been destroyed."
   Malachi 3:6

———

Therefore, if anyone is in Christ, he is a new creation; the old has passed away, and see, the new has come!
   2 Corinthians 5:17

———

Jesus Christ is the same yesterday, today, and forever.
   Hebrews 13:8

Lord Jesus, I do not know what the future holds for me, and it fills me with fear. I know that this grief is not the end of my story, and that You have a far greater plan ahead of me, but right now it is impossible for me to see. No matter what the future brings, may I take heart that You are with me until the end of the age. Bring me peace in the midst of this change, that I may not fear what is to come.

Amen

None of us are immune from hardships, loss, and grief, but we can take heart that no matter what has happened, the Lord promises to comfort us. Sometimes He comforts us directly, sometimes through circumstances, and sometimes through the people He places in our lives. Think about the ways that God has comforted you in your times of need.

Even when I go through the darkest valley, I fear no danger, for you are with me; your rod and your staff—they comfort me.

Psalm 23:4

———

Remember your word to your servant; you have given me hope through it. This is my comfort in my affliction: Your promise has given me life.

Psalm 119:49–50

———

As a mother comforts her son, so I will comfort you, and you will be comforted in Jerusalem.

Isaiah 66:13

Blessed are those who mourn, for they will be comforted.

    Matthew 5:4

————

Blessed be the God and Father of our Lord Jesus Christ, the Father of mercies and the God of all comfort. He comforts us in all our affliction, so that we may be able to comfort those who are in any kind of affliction, through the comfort we ourselves receive from God.

    2 Corinthians 1:3–4

Dear God, thank You for comforting me and healing my heart in times of trial. I am lost in my grief and I know that the only way out is with Your comforting hand. Thank You for putting people in my life who bring me comfort. Guide me to those whom You have chosen for me as kindred spirits. Guide my actions that I may be a source of comfort for others. Use my life as a blessing for others. Amen

At home, at work, in friendships, in families, in life—contentment is hard! We are constantly looking around to see what could be better, what we are missing out on, or what we used to have. The quickest route to contentment is through gratitude and trust; gratitude to God for what He has provided you, and trust that He will continue to give you everything you need. Recognize the goodness in your life. See the good, and trust that God never fails to provide for your needs.

*"So don't worry, saying, 'What will we eat?' or
'What will we drink?' or 'What will we wear?'
For the Gentiles eagerly seek all these things,
and your heavenly Father knows that you need
them. But seek first the kingdom of God and his
righteousness, and all these things will be provided
for you. Therefore don't worry about tomorrow,
because tomorrow will worry about itself. Each day
has enough trouble of its own."*

   Matthew 6:31–34

———

*But godliness with contentment is great gain. For
we brought nothing into the world, and we can take
nothing out. If we have food and clothing, we will
be content with these.*

   1 Timothy 6:6–8

*He then told them, "Watch out and be on guard
against all greed, because one's life is not in the
abundance of his possessions."*

    Luke 12:15

———

*I don't say this out of need, for I have learned to be
content in whatever circumstances I find myself.
I know both how to make do with little, and I
know how to make do with a lot. In any and all
circumstances I have learned the secret of being
content—whether well fed or hungry, whether in
abundance or in need.*

    Philippians 4:11–12

Heavenly Father, thank You for your unfailing love and faithfulness. Father, when I am lost in discontentment push me to see all that You have provided for me. Do not allow me to continue to be blind, but open my eyes to the goodness that surrounds me exactly where I am. Grow in me a godly contentment, never wishing I was anywhere but exactly where You have placed me. Amen

Having courage doesn't mean that you feel no fear; rather it means having a willingness and readiness to proceed despite the fear. It means working through your grief, knowing that even when you are at your worst, God is always at His best. Choose to have courage even when you feel destroyed, trusting that God is enough.

"Haven't I commanded you: be strong and courageous? Do not be afraid or discouraged, for the LORD your God is with you wherever you go."
> *Joshua 1:9*

———

I always let the LORD guide me. Because he is at my right hand, I will not be shaken.
> *Psalm 16:8*

———

Wait for the LORD; be strong, and let your heart be courageous. Wait for the LORD.
> *Psalm 27:14*

Be alert, stand firm in the faith, be courageous, be strong.

    1 Corinthians 16:13

———

For God has not given us a spirit of fear, but one of power, love, and sound judgment.

    2 Timothy 1:7

Dear God, grant me a sense of Your strength and presence that I may face this day and its challenges with courage. Do not allow me to despair or cower. No matter the obstacle, You are enough, and I have courage, not because of anything that I am capable of, but because of the confidence that I have in You. Amen

When your heart is heavy and your mind is burdened, hold fast to the truth that God comforts us in all of our afflictions so that we may be able to comfort others with His love. On our darkest days, Christ is there to lift us up into the light. When you find yourself lost in depression, allow these verses to fill your heart and bring you back to the truth.

The LORD sits enthroned over the flood; the LORD sits enthroned, King forever. The LORD gives his people strength; the LORD blesses his people with peace.

Psalm 29:10–11

———

The LORD is near the brokenhearted; he saves those crushed in spirit.

Psalm 34:18

———

Do not fear, for I am with you; do not be afraid, for I am your God. I will strengthen you; I will help you; I will hold on to you with my righteous right hand.

Isaiah 41:10

Answer me quickly, LORD; my spirit fails. Don't hide your face from me, or I will be like those going down to the Pit. Let me experience your faithful love in the morning, for I trust in you. Reveal to me the way I should go because I appeal to you.

   Psalm 143:7–8

———

I will give you the treasures of darkness and riches from secret places, so that you may know that I am the LORD. I am the God of Israel, who calls you by your name.

   Isaiah 45:3

Dear Jesus, You were a man of sorrows and acquainted with grief—please fill my heart with Your strength and peace. Meet me where I am, and help me to find the way back into the light. My spirit is crushed, but I know You have saved me and will continue to do so. Be my strength when I am weak, my joy when I have none, and my light when I wander in darkness. Amen

God places people in our lives for a reason and for our good. Seek out those who bring you encouragement. Pray for those you can bring encouragement to. Never hold in kindness that can be spread to lift up those around you. You never know when those words are God pouring out encouragement through you to others.

*The L*ord *is the one who will go before you. He will be with you; he will not leave you or abandon you. Do not be afraid or discouraged.*

Deuteronomy 31:8

———

God is our refuge and strength, a helper who is always found in times of trouble.

Psalm 46:1

———

Aren't five sparrows sold for two pennies? Yet not one of them is forgotten in God's sight. Indeed, the hairs of your head are all counted. Don't be afraid; you are worth more than many sparrows.

Luke 12:6–7

I have told you these things so that in me you may have peace. You will have suffering in this world. Be courageous! I have conquered the world.

    John 16:33

———

And let us watch out for one another to provoke love and good works, not neglecting to gather together, as some are in the habit of doing, but encouraging each other, and all the more as you see the day approaching.

    Hebrews 10:24–25

Christ Jesus, may Your Spirit strengthen and encourage my heart today. Comfort me in my grief, and lift me out of my discouraged state. Show me those around me who need my encouragement. Place on my heart those friends who need a kind word today. Allow me to be the tool You use to help lift up everyone I meet today. Amen

The tragic relativity of time is the speed with which an hour of joy passes, and the lifetime a moment of despair takes. But the truth is that our entire lives are just a mark on the time line of eternity. God is outside, above, and in control of all time. Though we walk through grief now, soon we will be with Him for all eternity.

Before the mountains were born, before you gave birth to the earth and the world, from eternity to eternity, you are God.

Psalm 90:2

———

He has made everything appropriate in its time. He has also put eternity in their hearts, but no one can discover the work God has done from beginning to end.

Ecclesiastes 3:11

———

This is eternal life: that they may know you, the only true God, and the one you have sent—Jesus Christ.

John 17:3

"Truly I tell you, anyone who hears my word and believes him who sent me has eternal life and will not come under judgment but has passed from death to life."

    John 5:24

———

For the wages of sin is death, but the gift of God is eternal life in Christ Jesus our Lord.

    Romans 6:23

Father, I know that this grief is only temporary, and soon I will be with You in heaven, but that does not make the pain of today feel any less real. God, take this pain away from me. Help me to see time through Your eyes. Grant me the patience to get through this season, and the wisdom to see Your plan. Give me a vision of heaven that brings me joy in knowing that I will get to spend all eternity there with You. Amen

God's everlasting faithfulness to His people is a deep source of hope, as well as an inspiration for how we should conduct ourselves in our relationships. No matter what we do, where we are, or what we are going through, God is faithful. He is steady, constant, prepared, and will be the strength that you need. Put your trust in Him, and you will never be betrayed.

Because of the LORD's faithful love we do not perish, for his mercies never end. They are new every morning; great is your faithfulness!
  Lamentations 3:22–23

———

"His master said to him, 'Well done, good and faithful servant! You were faithful over a few things; I will put you in charge of many things. Share your master's joy.'"
  Matthew 25:21

———

If we are faithless, he remains faithful, for he cannot deny himself.
  2 Timothy 2:13

Whoever is faithful in very little is also faithful in much, and whoever is unrighteous in very little is also unrighteous in much. So if you have not been faithful with worldly wealth, who will trust you with what is genuine? And if you have not been faithful with what belongs to someone else, who will give you what is your own?

   Luke 16:10–12

———

Let us hold on to the confession of our hope without wavering, since he who promised is faithful.

   Hebrews 10:23

Dear God, Lamentations is the perfect example of a people lost in their grief. Right now I am lost in my own grief. I am crying out to You and feel completely alone with what I am going through. Plant in my heart the words of Lamentations 3:22–23. Remind me every morning of Your new mercies. I know that You are faithful, and no matter what this life throws at me I will not perish under it because You are faithful. Amen

FEAR

Fear comes in many forms; fear of the unknown, of the impossible, of broken trust. Any of these fears can be all consuming. But we have an Almighty God who loves us and cares for us at all times. We have a powerful God who is strong through all things. We have an omnipresent God who never leaves us alone, and a God who is greater than any of our fears. With God on our side, there is nothing to fear, and nothing to stand in our way.

*Haven't I commanded you: be strong and
courageous? Do not be afraid or discouraged, for the
LORD your God is with you wherever you go.*
  Joshua 1:9

———

When I am afraid, I will trust in you.
  Psalm 56:3

———

*You did not receive a spirit of slavery to fall
back into fear. Instead, you received the Spirit of
adoption, by whom we cry out, "Abba, Father!"*
  Romans 8:15

For God has not given us a spirit of fear, but one of power, love, and sound judgment.

   2 Timothy 1:7

———

Humble yourselves, therefore, under the mighty hand of God, so that he may exalt you at the proper time, casting all your cares on him, because he cares about you.

   1 Peter 5:6–7

Abba, Father, I cry out to You for Your protection and comfort. I'm overwhelmed with fear. Fear of the future, and the unknown. I know that my fear stems from distrust, and that if I truly trusted You the way I say I do, then I would not have any fear.

Thank You for Your faithful love and comfort. Continue to shelter me when I feel afraid. Amen

Forgiving someone who has hurt you means you no longer call to mind their fault or error—this extends grace to them and freedom for you. But it is not something that comes naturally, or easily; especially when the hurt has been caused by someone you trusted. This level of forgiveness is only possible by leaning on the Holy Spirit within you and allowing Him to take control of cleaning your heart.

Therefore I tell you, her many sins have been forgiven; that's why she loved much. But the one who is forgiven little, loves little.

    Luke 7:47

———

Live in harmony with one another. Do not be proud; instead, associate with the humble. Do not be wise in your own estimation. Do not repay anyone evil for evil. Give careful thought to do what is honorable in everyone's eyes. If possible, as far as it depends on you, live at peace with everyone.

    Romans 12:16–18

Be kind and compassionate to one another, forgiving one another, just as God also forgave you in Christ.

Ephesians 4:32

———

As God's chosen ones, holy and dearly loved, put on compassion, kindness, humility, gentleness, and patience, bearing with one another and forgiving one another if anyone has a grievance against another. Just as the Lord has forgiven you, so you are also to forgive.

Colossians 3:12–13

Dear God, it is easy for me to say that I forgive someone, but to actually release the resentment from my heart and let it be as if nothing ever happened . . . well I do not have any idea how to do that. Sometimes I feel trapped by the grudges and feelings of hurt that I have chosen to hold on to. I know that the feelings are not only damaging me, but my relationships as well. Please, just as you forgave all my debts and wrongs through Christ, empower me to extend forgiveness to those who have mistreated or hurt me. Amen

What do you see when you look into your future? Do you see happiness? Grief? Fear? A sparkling cloud of the unknown? No matter what feelings the idea of your future bring about, remember that the Lord is holding it in His hands and has greater plans for you than you could ever imagine for yourself. Leave your future at His feet, and focus on what He has for you today.

The LORD *will fulfill his purpose for me.* LORD, *your faithful love endures forever; do not abandon the work of your hands.*

> *Psalm 138:8*

———

A person's heart plans his way, but the LORD *determines his steps.*

> *Proverbs 16:9*

———

"For I know the plans I have for you"—this is the LORD's *declaration—"plans for your well-being, not for disaster, to give you a future and a hope."*

> *Jeremiah 29:11*

But our citizenship is in heaven, and we eagerly wait for a Savior from there, the Lord Jesus Christ. He will transform the body of our humble condition into the likeness of his glorious body, by the power that enables him to subject everything to himself.

Philippians 3:20–21

———

Dear friends, we are God's children now, and what we will be has not yet been revealed. We know that when he appears, we will be like him because we will see him as he is.

1 John 3:2

Father, the future is the great unknown. My desire for control makes me fear my carefully laid plans not working out, but I know that ultimately You are the only One who can plan my future. Grant me patience to wait for Your plan to unfold in Your timing, and continue to be patient with me as I stumble trying to make my own path. Thank You for being worthy of my trust, and for the future that You have planned for me. Amen

Grace is not deserved. It is not needed by the person who has always been reliable, or the child who has never been in trouble. The one who needs your grace is the friend who has cancelled on you four times this week, and now needs your help; the spouse who went on a shopping spree and forgot your birthday; the neighbor who complains about your lawn to others, and now needs help raking. How can you possibly bestow grace on these people? By the grace you have received from the Creator of the universe, you have the power to pass that grace on to others. The greatest gift we will ever receive is grace—the wholly unmerited favor of the Most High. Allow that grace to flow out of you to those who deserve it the least.

The law came along to multiply the trespass. But where sin multiplied, grace multiplied even more.
    Romans 5:20

———

For sin will not rule over you, because you are not under the law but under grace.
    Romans 6:14

———

Now if by grace, then it is not by works; otherwise grace ceases to be grace.
    Romans 11:6

But he said to me, "My grace is sufficient for you, for my power is perfected in weakness." Therefore, I will most gladly boast all the more about my weaknesses, so that Christ's power may reside in me.

   2 Corinthians 12:9

———

For you are saved by grace through faith, and this is not from yourselves; it is God's gift—not from works, so that no one can boast.

   Ephesians 2:8–9

Lord God, thank You for Your riches of grace that have been poured out on me through faith in Christ Jesus. I am left speechless when I think about all the repeated sin in my life that You have wiped clean. I know I do not deserve any of it, and yet Your grace abounds. Help me to show that level of grace to the people in my life. I know that only with Your strength will I be able to repay those who have sinned against me with grace. Amen

The deep sorrow of grief that comes from losing a loved one, a longtime friend, or even a pet can seem profound and unending—but God promises to be near us, to comfort us, and to bring joy and beauty out of the ashes. That sounds great, but how do you find that comfort and joy in the midst of your sorrow? Spend time in prayer. Saturate yourself in Scripture. Meditate on His words, and He will bring you comfort you could never have imagined.

The righteous cry out, and the L<small>ORD</small> hears, and rescues them from all their troubles. The L<small>ORD</small> is near the brokenhearted; he saves those crushed in spirit.

Psalm 34:17–18

––––––

Why, my soul, are you so dejected? Why are you in such turmoil? Put your hope in God, for I will still praise him, my Savior and my God.

Psalm 42:5

––––––

So you also have sorrow now. But I will see you again. Your hearts will rejoice, and no one will take away your joy from you.

John 16:22

Then the young women will rejoice with dancing,
while young and old men rejoice together. I
will turn their mourning into joy, give them
consolation, and bring happiness out of grief.
   Jeremiah 31:13

———

Though the fig tree does not bud and there is no
fruit on the vines, though the olive crop fails
and the fields produce no food, though the flocks
disappear from the pen and there are no herds in
the stalls, yet I will celebrate in the Lord; I will
rejoice in the God of my salvation!
   Habakkuk 3:17–18

Heavenly Father, my heart is aching and all I see is darkness. I am alone and lost. I know that there is no way out on my own. I trust that You are my light and my salvation, and that You can pull me out of the valley I find myself in. Father, hold me in Your arms and let me feel Your warmth. Give the rest my heart so desperately needs to heal. Lead me to still waters that I may be at peace during this time of chaos. My heart is Yours to mold. Amen

It's tempting to put our hope in the wrong places—relationships, financial security, personal or professional abilities—but all of these will let us down and leave us broken. Our firmest hope is found only in Christ Jesus. He is our rock and firm foundation. When we are at the bottom, we know that ultimately He will save us from our brokenness and bring us back into the light.

But those who trust in the LORD *will renew their strength; they will soar on wings like eagles; they will run and not become weary, they will walk and not faint.*

    Isaiah 40:31

———

I wait for the LORD*; I wait and put my hope in his word.*

    Psalm 130:5

———

Now may the God of hope fill you with all joy and peace as you believe so that you may overflow with hope by the power of the Holy Spirit.

    Romans 15:13

We have also obtained access through him by faith into this grace in which we stand, and we rejoice in the hope of the glory of God. And not only that, but we also rejoice in our afflictions, because we know that affliction produces endurance, endurance produces proven character, and proven character produces hope.

Romans 5:2–4

———

Let us run with endurance the race that lies before us, keeping our eyes on Jesus, the source and perfecter of our faith. For the joy that lay before him, he endured the cross, despising the shame, and sat down at the right hand of the throne of God. For consider him who endured such hostility from sinners against himself, so that you won't grow weary and give up.

Hebrews 12:1b–3

Lord of hope, please fill me with all joy and peace as I hope in You. Hope is difficult when I am stuck in the midst of grief, and I know that it is only You that can give me the hope I need to find Your overflowing joy. Father, where grief dwells, Your hope abounds. Let my cup be so filled with hope, that no matter what hits me, only hope will pour out. Amen

Even surrounded by people, it is easy to feel alone. Thanks to social media, and the fast pace of modern life, many of us are left feeling isolated—but thanks to God's faithful presence and our community of believers, we never have to be alone. Jesus will never leave you, or cancel plans. He is always available for you when you need Him. When you are lost in your grief, Jesus is right next to you ready to sit with you as long as you need, and pull you up when you are ready.

My presence will go with you, and I will give you rest.

   Exodus 33:14

———

The LORD is the one who will go before you. He will be with you; he will not leave you or abandon you. Do not be afraid or discouraged.

   Deuteronomy 31:8

———

God provides homes for those who are deserted. He leads out the prisoners to prosperity, but the rebellious live in a scorched land.

   Psalm 68:6

He heals the brokenhearted and bandages their wounds.

Psalm 147:3

———

Blessed be the God and Father of our Lord Jesus Christ, the Father of mercies and the God of all comfort. He comforts us in all our affliction, so that we may be able to comfort those who are in any kind of affliction, through the comfort we ourselves receive from God.

2 Corinthians 1:3–4

Father of mercies, please comfort me in these times of loneliness so that I may be a comfort to others. Remind me that even in my deepest despair, no matter where I am, You are with me. Thank You for being a constant reminder that I am never alone. Continue to hold me in Your arms, and help me to be a shoulder for others to help them know that I am here for them. Amen

Our highest calling is to love God with all of our heart, our soul, and our mind, and to love our neighbor as ourselves. But what does it mean to love our neighbor as ourselves? It is easy to love our friends, but enemies are a whole other story. Only with God's love in our hearts are we able to truly love all people.

*But I say to you who listen: Love your enemies, do
what is good to those who hate you, bless those who
curse you, pray for those who mistreat you.*

Luke 6:27–28

———

*Love is patient, love is kind. Love does not envy, is
not boastful, is not arrogant, is not rude, is not self-
seeking, is not irritable, and does not keep a record
of wrongs.*

1 Corinthians 13:4–5

———

*Above all, maintain constant love for one another,
since love covers a multitude of sins.*

1 Peter 4:8

God's love was revealed among us in this way: God sent his one and only Son into the world so that we might live through him.

1 John 4:9

———

And we have come to know and to believe the love that God has for us. God is love, and the one who remains in love remains in God, and God remains in him.

1 John 4:16

Dear Jesus, there are people in my life that it is hard for me to love. I know that I am still called to love them, but it seems impossible without Your guidance. Instill in my heart the selfless concern and compassion for others that You demonstrated for me. Help me to love people with Your love, and not with what I am capable of on my own. Amen

When the demands of life overwhelm you, remember that you can approach God's throne of grace with boldness because of the mercy that he has granted you. But how can you pass that mercy on to others? When your spirit is grieved, do not allow it to cause hatred for those that have caused it. Pray for God to grant you the strength to give mercy to those who do not deserve it, and forgive those who have caused you grief.

Blessed are the merciful, for they will be shown mercy.

   Matthew 5:7

———

"Go and learn what this means: I desire mercy and not sacrifice. For I didn't come to call the righteous, but sinners."

   Matthew 9:13

———

Therefore, let us approach the throne of grace with boldness, so that we may receive mercy and find grace to help us in time of need.

   Hebrews 4:16

Speak and act as those who are to be judged by the law of freedom. For judgment is without mercy to the one who has not shown mercy. Mercy triumphs over judgment.

James 2:12–13

———

Blessed be the God and Father of our Lord Jesus Christ. Because of his great mercy he has given us new birth into a living hope through the resurrection of Jesus Christ from the dead.

1 Peter 1:3

Lord God, thank You for Your mercy and lovingkindness in times of need. I know that I have grieved Your heart and am undeserving of the compassion that You have bestowed upon me by giving me mercy. I am not strong enough to be merciful to those who have hurt me. Father, let Your mercy flow through me, that I may forgive those who I would never be able to forgive on my own. Amen

If you are at peace in all of your relationships, it is only a matter of time before conflict will arise. Rather than worry over what has happened in the past or what might happen in the future, be still with the Lord in the peace of the present moment. Be the one to ask for forgiveness, rather than holding on to resentment. Make the first step toward peace.

You will keep the mind that is dependent on you in perfect peace, for it is trusting in you.

   Isaiah 26:3

———

For I am persuaded that neither death nor life, nor angels nor rulers, nor things present nor things to come, nor powers, nor height nor depth, nor any other created thing will be able to separate us from the love of God that is in Christ Jesus our Lord.

   Romans 8:38–39

Peace I leave with you. My peace I give to you. I do not give to you as the world gives. Don't let your heart be troubled or fearful.

　John 14:27

———

And the peace of God, which surpasses all understanding, will guard your hearts and minds in Christ Jesus. Finally brothers and sisters, whatever is true, whatever is honorable, whatever is just, whatever is pure, whatever is lovely, whatever is commendable—if there is any moral excellence and if there is anything praiseworthy—dwell on these things.

　Philippians 4:7–8

Lord Jesus, I feel chaos and conflict in so many areas of my life. It is easy for me to be caught in the mess and forget the perfect peace that You have laid out for me. May Your perfect peace guard my heart and mind as I trust in You. Grant me the humility to seek out peace and be the one to lay down my pride at the feet of conflict, that my relationships may be redeemed. Amen

There are many ways to praise the Lord God beyond singing songs in church—when you live from a place of love and gratitude, your entire life becomes an act of praise and worship. That can be an easy thing to do when you are happy, but when your heart grieves it can be hard to find words of praise. Whatever state your heart is in, God is no less worthy of your praise. Praise Him in your grief for His comforting and ever-present hand in Your life. Praise Him for who He is, and because He is worthy.

*I will praise God's name with song and exalt him
with thanksgiving.*

    Psalm 69:30

———

*Hallelujah! Praise God in his sanctuary. Praise him
in his mighty expanse. Praise him for his powerful
acts; praise him for his abundant greatness.*

    Psalm 150:1–2

For from him and through him and to him are all things. To him be the glory forever. Amen.

Romans 11:36

———

Now to him who is able to protect you from stumbling and to make you stand in the presence of his glory, without blemish and with great joy, to the only God our Savior, through Jesus Christ our Lord, be glory, majesty, power, and authority before all time, now and forever. Amen.

Jude 24–25

Lord Jesus, from You and through You and to You are all things—to You be the glory forever and ever. I praise You for Your strength and power. For Your ability to pull me through the valley, when I want to fall down. I praise You for Your grace in forgiving my aching heart. I praise You for all that You are and all that You have done. Amen

In the same way that our friendships and relationships with people need communication to be strengthened, so does our relationship with God. He has blessed us with the ability to speak to Him at all times, whenever we need Him. Especially when we are lost in grief, the best gift is dedicated time with our Creator. No matter how we come to the Lord, whether to present our requests or to sit silently in His presence, we can trust that He hears us.

"*Whenever you pray, you must not be like the hypocrites, because they love to pray standing in the synagogues and on the street corners to be seen by people. . . . But when you pray, go into your private room, shut your door, and pray to your Father who is in secret. And your Father who sees in secret will reward you. When you pray, don't babble like the Gentiles, since they imagine they'll be heard for their many words. . . .*

"*Therefore, you should pray like this: Our Father in heaven, your name be honored as holy. Your kingdom come. Your will be done on earth as it is in heaven. Give us today our daily bread. And forgive us our debts, as we also have forgiven our debtors. And do not bring us into temptation, but deliver us from the evil one.*

"*For if you forgive others their offenses, your heavenly Father will forgive you as well. But if you don't forgive others, your Father will not forgive your offenses.*"

Matthew 6:5–15

If you remain in me and my words remain in you,
ask whatever you want and it will be done for you.
    John 15:7

————

In the same way the Spirit also helps us in our
weakness, because we do not know what to pray for
as we should, but the Spirit himself intercedes for
us with unspoken groanings.
    Romans 8:26

————

Don't worry about anything, but in everything,
through prayer and petition with thanksgiving,
present your requests to God.
    Philippians 4:6

Lord Jesus, just as You taught Your followers how to pray, instill in me a deep desire to seek Your presence. Send reminders into my life of my need to spend time with You. Help me to remember to not only speak in my prayers, but to sit and listen to what You have to say to me. Give me rest in Your presence, that my spirit may be healed. Amen

Our security and peace comes from the Lord, who is our strong tower and refuge. God's protection over His children is difficult for us to understand, because He does not always answer our prayers of protection in the ways that we would expect. But we always trust that His will is greater than our own, and ultimately His plan will be good for those that He calls His children.

Protect me as the pupil of your eye; hide me in the shadow of your wings.

Psalm 17:8

———

The angel of the LORD encamps around those who fear him, and rescues them.

Psalm 34:7

———

The mountains surround Jerusalem and the LORD surrounds his people, both now and forever.

Psalm 125:2

The name of the LORD is a strong tower; the righteous run to it and are protected.

Proverbs 18:10

———

But the Lord is faithful; he will strengthen and guard you from the evil one.

2 Thessalonians 3:3

Heavenly Father, please watch over me and my loved ones. Keep us safe both from physical and supernatural attacks. Direct us away from danger and destruction. When I find myself in fear, ease my heart and let me feel Your presence. Amen

Our deepest purpose is not in what we do but in who we are—people who love, honor, and praise the only One who is worthy. It is the purpose that each of us was created for, to glorify God.

*When all has been heard, the conclusion of the
matter is this: fear God and keep his commands,
because this is for all humanity.*
    Ecclesiastes 12:13

———

*My Father is glorified by this: that you produce
much fruit and prove to be my disciples.*
    John 15:8

———

*But I consider my life of no value to myself; my
purpose is to finish my course and the ministry I
received from the Lord Jesus, to testify to the gospel
of God's grace.*
    Acts 20:24

He has saved us and called us with a holy calling, not according to our works, but according to his own purpose and grace, which was given to us in Christ Jesus before time began.

    2 Timothy 1:9

———

Sing to him; sing praise to him; tell about all his wondrous works! Honor his holy name; let the hearts of those who seek the L<small>ORD</small> rejoice.

    1 Chronicles 16:9–10

Lord Jesus, may each day offer me opportunities to live out my true purpose by loving and serving You, and those around me who were created in Your image. Guide my steps down the path You have created for me, that I may glorify You in all that I do. Amen

Accepting God's sovereignty can feel like giving up control, but in reality it is giving up the chains we have allowed ourselves to be wrapped in, and living in the freedom that is only available by those that trust God's plan. We trust in God's sovereignty because He is the Creator of the universe and sustains all things by His powerful Word.

The LORD does whatever he pleases in heaven and
on earth, in the seas and all the depths.
Psalm 135:6

———

A person's heart plans his way, but the LORD
determines his steps.
Proverbs 16:9

———

A king's heart is like channeled water in the LORD's
hand: He directs it wherever he chooses.
Proverbs 21:1

What should we say then? Is there injustice with God? Absolutely not! For he tells Moses, I will show mercy to whom I will show mercy, and I will have compassion on whom I will have compassion. So then, it does not depend on human will or effort but on God who shows mercy. For the Scripture tells Pharaoh, I raised you up for this reason so that I may display my power in you and that my name may be proclaimed in the whole earth. So then, he has mercy on whom he wants to have mercy and he hardens whom he wants to harden.

    Romans 9:14–18

———

We know that all things work together for the good of those who love God, who are called according to his purpose.

    Romans 8:28

My good and faithful God, may my heart and soul rest in knowing that You uphold the world and Your purposes cannot be thwarted. Ease my fearful heart, and help me to release the control I try to hold on to over my life. Grant me the freedom of trusting that Your plans are greater than anything I could come up with on my own. Amen

Strength comes in different forms. There is, of course, physical strength, but there is also strength of spirit, strength of intellect, and even emotional strength. In all of these areas, eventually we will fail. The weight will become too much, and you will break. But we do not hold our own weight. God can hold everything we are holding on to, and more. There is nothing that is too much for Him to handle. He is our ultimate strength, and if we truly pass all of the weight to Him, we will never fail.

But he said to me, "My grace is sufficient for you, for my power is perfected in weakness." Therefore, I will most gladly boast all the more about my weaknesses, so that Christ's power may reside in me. So I take pleasure in weaknesses, insults, hardships, persecutions, and in difficulties, for the sake of Christ. For when I am weak, then I am strong.

　　2 Corinthians 12:9–10

———

If I say, "My foot is slipping," your faithful love will support me, LORD.

　　Psalm 94:18

My flesh and my heart may fail, but God is the strength of my heart, my portion forever.
Psalm 73:26

———

Consider it a great joy, my brothers and sisters, whenever you experience various trials, because you know that the testing of your faith produces endurance.
James 1:2–3

Father, I am weak! I am falling apart in my grief. I have walked as far as I can, and I can go no farther. But You do not leave me to my own strength. You lift me up off the ground and carry me down the path. I know I would not make it on my strength alone, but I also know that with Your strength there is nothing I cannot get through. There is nothing that is too great for You to overcome. Give me the humility to pass my load fully to You. With You as my strength I will be victorious. Amen

When you are in a pit of grief, it can be difficult to find things to be grateful for. But the more we practice gratitude and thanksgiving, the more abundance and goodness we recognize all around us. Even on your lowest day, find ways to thank God.

Give thanks to the LORD, for he is good; his faithful love endures forever.

Psalm 118:1

———

For we know that the one who raised the Lord Jesus will also raise us with Jesus and present us with you. Indeed, everything is for your benefit so that, as grace extends through more and more people, it may cause thanksgiving to increase to the glory of God.

2 Corinthians 4:14–16

Rejoice always, pray constantly, give thanks in everything; for this is God's will for you in Christ Jesus.

   1 Thessalonians 5:16–18

———

Every good and perfect gift is from above, coming down from the Father of lights, who does not change like shifting shadows.

   James 1:17

Father, I praise You and thank You for every good and perfect gift You have given. I thank You for Your constant comfort and guiding light. Help me to never lose sight of Your blessings. Sooth my aching soul and show me how to glorify You through my suffering. Amen

Trust is not an easy thing to give away. Everyone has had a time when their trust has been given to a friend, only to be betrayed. But God is not a fallible human. To trust the Lord is to believe what He has said about Himself: He is good, faithful, and sovereign. He is always worthy and deserving of our trust.

The person who trusts in the Lord, *whose confidence indeed is the* Lord, *is blessed. He will be like a tree planted by water: it sends its roots out toward a stream, it doesn't fear when heat comes, and its foliage remains green. It will not worry in a year of drought or cease producing fruit.*

Jeremiah 17:7–8

———

Wait for the Lord; *be strong, and let your heart be courageous. Wait for the* Lord.

Psalm 27:14

———

And my God will supply all your needs according to his riches in glory in Christ Jesus.

Philippians 4:19

I will be with you when you pass through the waters, and when you pass through the rivers, they will not overwhelm you. You will not be scorched when you walk through the fire, and the flame will not burn you.

    Isaiah 43:2

––––––

This is the confidence we have before him: If we ask anything according to his will, he hears us.

    1 John 5:14

Dear God, thank You for working all things together for the good of those who love You and are called according to Your purpose. Thank You for being worthy of my trust and forgiving me when I question You. I praise Your matchless faithfulness. Help my disbelief. Amen

Worry is false and useless fear—it's imagining and anticipating what might happen but probably won't. What can you change by worrying about it? Nothing. What can you fix by thinking about everything that could go wrong? Nothing. Instead, spend your time focused on today, on what you can do, on what you know to be truth, and leave the rest to God.

"Therefore I tell you: Don't worry about your life, what you will eat or what you will drink; or about your body, what you will wear. Isn't life more than food and the body more than clothing? Consider the birds of the sky: They don't sow or reap or gather into barns, yet your heavenly Father feeds them. Aren't you worth more than they? Can any of you add one moment to his life-span by worrying?"

  Matthew 6:25–27

———

The Lord answered her, "Martha, Martha, you are worried and upset about many things, but one thing is necessary. Mary has made the right choice, and it will not be taken away from her."

  Luke 10:41–42

We know that all things work together for the good of those who love God, who are called according to his purpose.

   Romans 8:28

———

Don't worry about anything, but in everything, through prayer and petition with thanksgiving, present your requests to God. And the peace of God, which surpasses all understanding, will guard your hearts and minds in Christ Jesus.

   Philippians 4:6–7

Lord Jesus, I am often worried about many things. I worry about tomorrow, about my family, about what friends are really thinking, about health, about clothes, about money, and about countless other meaningless things. Jesus, I know that my worry will do nothing, but the thoughts are rooted in my mind, and I know I cannot remove them without Your help. Remind me of Your provision. Show me ways to let go of my worry. Please grant me a heart like Mary, who rested at Your feet. Amen

VERSE INDEX